Of Love & Other Dirty Business

Ottis Blades

Copyright @ Ottis Blades
Bohemian Soul Publishing.
2016, All Rights Reserved.

Cover by Gabrielle Ayers

ISBN-13:978-0692690611
ISBN-10:0692690611

Dedication:

This book is dedicated to the muses who made it possible to be written. In the name of love and indifference, heartache and desolation, empty dinner plates and abandon. I drink to you, and your cute angry pouts. Always.

With her Florentino Ariza learned what he had already experienced many times without realizing it: that one can be in love with several people at the same time, feel the same sorrow with each, and not betray any of them. Alone in the midst of the crowd on the pier, he said to himself in a flash of anger: 'My heart has more rooms than a whorehouse.'

-Gabriel Garcia Marquez,
Love In The Time Of Cholera

Before We Get Started...

...Where do I start? If I were to say that I've been working on this book for a long time, I would be lying, maybe a bit more than usual, maybe making more things up to write about as I go along, but before my train of thought runs away with this introduction, I'd like to admit that I was never working on this book. The past few years I have been working on a short story collection titled "Restless Souls Sleep together" but who knows when that'll see the light of day. See, I got distracted by this social media application called Instagram, used by hipsters to show off their cool nature pics, and attention-starved girls trying to get a modeling career off the ground. There's also a community of writers there, and some of them write little quotes on typewriters much to the delight of many, others have no idea what they're doing and a handful are ridiculously good. In short, it's like finding the Smurf Village amidst all the crazy memes and other distractions the online world has to offer. So, what does all this have to do with anything, you may ask? Well, for starters, the following pieces of literature, or whatever you want to call them, I don't care, come directly from my IG account, written exclusively to fit that small dank square users are afforded. In doing so, it became kind of a challenge to write a short cohesive story without saying much, but still be able to grip the heart and make puppies cry. I like calling these pieces "miniature short stories disguised as poetry" or something of the like, and they're meant to be read as a stream of consciousness because that's the way they were written in the past six months with the backdrop of whiskey, tons of beer, 1970s rock 'n roll and resisting the urge to drunk-dial an ex on most nights. So, yeah, I'm the cliché bohemian poet as you've probably figured out by now, and the stories you'll read in this book are condensed episodes of personal experiences, the everyday hardships of surroundings all too surreal, inventive creative fuckery and overall madness, but let's just call them a work of fiction and chalk them up to the imagination of the writer just in case. The title of this book is a tribute to Gabriel Garcia Marquez's *Of Love And Other Demons*, whose work is highly referenced throughout my writings. In conclusion, I'm glad this book is finally published so I can go back to finishing my short story collection before I get distracted again. Oooh, what is this Snapchat thing about?

-Ottis Blades
April 10, 2016

On With The Show

Sometimes I Poet but Not Today

Sitting Around in Circles	14
Disheveled Bohemian	15
Jersey City	16
Writing While Writing	17
A Fist Kiss	18
Of Booty Calls & Gas Money	19
Some Most Nights	20
Stay Still and Talk to Me	21
The Most Tiring of Summers	22
I Miss You a Little Bit Less	23
My Favorite	24
Be Good, Josh!	25
Another Love Letter to Love	26
Atlantic Philly/Miami City	27
Spoonful of Loving	28
Bear Mountain Beauty	29
And That's How She Slays	30
Butterflied Stomach	31
Chocolate Girl of Grapefruit Lips	32
Once Upon a Pig	33
You Looked So F'N Pretty Today	34
Twice Upon a Time in Mexico	35
Rewriting the Cold War	36
Pink Hoodie	37
Fight of the Century	38
Doing Her Dirty Laundry	39
Maybe the One	40
Gypsy Eyes	41

The Collateral of a Failed Relationship

Twitchy	44
6Av Blues	45
The Jig is Up	46
The End of Ends	47
Kissing In-Between Kissing	48
On Wasted Time	49
Things We Liked	50
Sunday Morning Breakfast	51
Handsome, Sexy Man	52
The Final Stop	53
Breaking Up, Breaking Down	54
Plight of the Coward	55
The Poems I Still Write	56
14th Street…Back for Me	57
3,722 Emails and None of Them Yours	58
Because I Still	59
Space Oddity	60
Trading Numbers	61
All We'll Have is Pictures	62
As it Turns Out…	63
Wedding Crashers	64
A Very Bohemian Christmas	65
It's Been a Minute Since Forever Ago	66
Going Back Home	67
Happenstance by the Pool	68
Goodnight, Babe	69
Of Love & Other Dirty Business	70

Of Other Dirty Business

The Drunk Poet Drives	74
Atlantic City Part 1	75
My 25th Hour	76
1950s Americana	77
Thankful for Abandoned Airports	78
I Don't Care About Things When I Do	79
95 South in the Way of Thanksgiving	80
Kim's Alley Bar	81
Atlantic City Part 2	82
New JersEngland	83
There's a Creeper in Your Inbox	84
Going Through Things	85
Slow Down, Take it Easy	86
A Sexting Buddy	87
Atlantic City Part 3	88
A Couple of Kids Watching Porn	89
Lonely Guy	90
Sleepless in A.C	91
Rejecting Heaven	92
Embracing Hell	93
Colored Chalk off the Asphalt	94
In a World...	95
And Then We Pray	96
Atlantic City Again	97
Growing up Without Feet	98
Women for All Seasons	99
A Day Without Poetry	100

The Rest Of What's Left

Another First Kiss	103
Ode to the Girl	104
Let's Talk About Sex	105
There's a War Coming	106
Ottis' Shitty Valentine's	107
All the Stops Along the Way	108
I'd Love to See You Again	109
I Love How You Selfie	110
Why Are You Forgetting Me?	111
How Much It Takes	112
Her Troops at My Door	113
Something to Write About	114
The College Look	115
Of Bohemian Dress & Bouncy Curls	116
Not Knowing a Thing About You	117
Another One for Aussie	118
Are You Okay?	119
Salads Cracking up	120
Through the Eyes of a Poet	121
She Loved My Poems but Not Much Else	122
A Good Woman	123
Love's Evil Magic	124
A Happy Couple	125
Growing up Spanish	126
She's You	127
MySpace & Yours	128
Something to Be Excited About	129

Round 1:

Sometimes I Poet But Not Today

Sitting Around in Circles

They'd sit around in a circle and sip their rum, often playing dominoes, sometimes not, but they always had stories to tell and souring music playing, battering their spirits. I'm talking about my dad, grandpa, and friends shooting the shit. I'd pick up my dad's cup and smell that disgusting smell and wonder what the fuck adults saw in it. Perhaps reflections of their past mistakes? And I watched as their faces gradually changed from jolly to trashed throughout the day and into the night, looking into my own future in my dad's glazed eyes. Now I sit in a circle, sometimes not, and sip on rum with the guys and shoot the shit and write some stuff. My kid looks at me with the same curious eyes I saw my dad with, disgusted by the scent of the rum and that's how I know: we are a copy of a copy of a copy, life repeating itself and manifesting a sobering note. We are connected souls whenever dad's ghost brings on the night, and turns off the day.

Disheveled Bohemian

Her eyes were Farrah Fawcett green, slinging drinks behind a bar in the worst part of town. She had all the drunks smitten, she was an emerald amongst those who couldn't distinguish gold from fugazy. She'd get love letters, marriage proposals, swooning regulars, and…me. Back then I roamed the city disheveled and unkempt. My girl had left me a few weeks earlier and I was using alcohol to climb back amongst the living. Yeah, I wasn't much to look at, but her deep forest eyes saw me and my beer gut as a chiseled Greek god, setting them ablaze. She'd pause for a moment, stare and say, "God you have the nicest lips." She'd toss me a wink, blow me a kiss, and I'd smile and blush like a 12-year-old. I'd write poems on napkins like, "I've never met beauty, until beauty introduced me to you." Fucking smooth. She loved those things. I'd leave for a bit and then come back at close. I'd have breakfast waiting for her at home, then we'd put the night to sleep in the twilight of love from 7 to 2. And that was every weekend until she went back to Greece, plunging the lost city of Atlantic City back into the ocean of misery from which it came.

Jersey City

Sigh, here we go. Wake up at a quarter to 8, shower, grab your stuff, walk a block up to Kennedy Boulevard, catch the cramped "immigrant bus" by 8:30, get off at Journal Square, walk into Hudson County Community College, power nap through a couple of classes, leave by 3, walk another block, take the path train to New York City, get off at 14th, stroll into work at 4, show off your pseudo culinary skills to the Haitian chef who always talked about his dick, get reprimanded for misplacing the funny bone, get off 9 hours later smelling like spiced duck anus, pick up a 6-pack at the corner, walk down the subway just in time to witness a hobo pull his pants down and take a dump, get on the 1:20 packed-as-balls path train, try to squeeze between hot chicks if possible, arrive by 2AM at Journal Square, get on the last bus, get off at Kennedy & Woodlawn, walk down half a block, get home, take a hot shower, light up the hookah, have a drink, knock out, get up by 7:45AM, time to do it again.

Writing While Writing

At the risk of sounding repetitive, it's the most nagging question of the day, don't ever ask me what I'm doing for you already know the answer: I'm writing. Let me rephrase that: I'm ALWAYS writing. I'm writing while at work, pen logged behind my ear and pockets full of notes. I'm writing at the movies, on a date with rum & coke. I'm writing on the john thinking of what's her face. I'm writing in my head. I'm writing in the shower. Hell, I'm writing this piece in my head while I'm in the shower. I'm writing in my sleep. I'm writing when I'm dancing. I'm even writing when I'm writing. I'm writing while you speak, and sure as shit can't wait to be done writing these honest words, only so I can start writing again some fucking more.

A First Kiss

You've got this, little one. Don't act like you've never felt this before. I'm not talking about the tired butterflies everyone else has, but the parasites scavenging your stomach because of eating too much sugar, or so grandma says, but this isn't time to believe her crazy stories. Listen, you're 12 years old now! A handsome young man! Wearing your hair neatly slicked back on Sundays to go with your best threads – the Reebok Pump sneakers and the TMNT sweater Mom sent from the states. So, why are you so nervous? It was only a few weeks ago crazy Maria from the corner shoved her tongue down your throat, so you already know how this will feel, more or less. You got practice time in, so man up! Show up at her door and bring some damn flowers – steal them from the neighbor if you must! Her mom will think it's cute! And go look into her dreamy eyes and tell her that you like her with no stutter in your voice. Be confident and assertive, your balls already dropped along with your heart the very moment she smiled back and took the initiative of taking you by the hand and kissing you, leaving the fresh scent of spring on your breath, because you graduated to summer then, and for as long as you live you won't be able to look at life and women the same way after.

Of Booty Calls & Gas Money

Got money for gas? Check. So what if the only break you get is the 25-minute drive from one job to the next? Got food in your tummy? Check. The *Arroz Con Pollo* mother brought earlier should hold you up for a few. Rent is due tomorrow? Fuck. But until your pen is able to cash the checks your mouth is writing, you still have a few more days to make due. No longer have a girlfriend? That's okay, you'll survive. Is the booty call still coming over with a 6-pack of Heineken and greasy Chinese? Atta boy! Now shut the fuck up and be thankful for whatever you have left. There are people on the internet going to bed thirsty and starving.

Some Most Nights

Some most nights I don't feel as handsome. I don't feel as good-looking and I don't feel much like being modest to be honest. I do feel as ugly, I feel downtrodden, abandoned, unwell, and defeated. I do feel alone, alone, and alone. Sometimes I don't feel like me, but I feel like them, like they do, like shit, like ass, and I'm not all right, and I don't feel like anything, I feel like hurt, I feel like pain, I feel like death, not as handsome, twice as ugly, and most of all alone, alone, and alone like them, like me, like you.

Stay Still and Talk to Me

All I want is for you to do one thing for me – stay still, look me in the eye, and just talk, and don't stop, and go, fast, go slow, however you'd like, and just talk to me, about anything. Think of something, a story you've been hiding, an anecdote that's yet to cross your mind during our countless pillow talks that never found any sleep and talk about us, our future, where do you see us 5 years from now? Maybe 6 months? A week? Or maybe go back to your childhood and dreams we've yet to wake up from. Just talk to me, woman, and let the fluidity of your mouth in motion take control. You're fluent in many tongues including my own, and that's when I want to sneak in a kiss, right in-between your tales of happiness and despair, your misadventures of doing never-ending laundry, your shitty boss, what's for dinner, and every single detail about your day that goes over my head, that's where I'd like to stop your breath for a second with the index finger on your pretty lips, and tell you that the greatest pleasure in my life is hearing you speak, to know that you're here, and that you're the reason I'm sitting across from you, still breathing. Now, if you would only shut the fuck up a minute and let me get a word in: I love you. Okay, that was three.

The Most Tiring of Summers

It was the most tiring of summers. I held two jobs and no car. She'd come to my place with the first morning rays and love my heart awake. Then, she'd drive me to work. I'd get off at 4 and commute on the bus to the next one. She'd pick me up at 10 and drop me back off at my place and then love my heart to sleep. Thank God neither of their husbands ever found out. I held 4 jobs that summer – and it nearly killed me.

I Miss You a Little Bit Less

The fact of the matter is this: I miss you a little bit less nowadays, but as tragedy would have it, I love you a little bit more still, for the heart grows fonder of the past even if I no longer think about you as much, and the months pile up and the calendar burns down, and the years since your departure free-fall from beyond and onto my solitude, threatening to crush me, but I just can't let it happen 'cause the truth is, I miss you a little bit less even if I love you a little bit more still, and Saturdays come and go and I don't even notice them, 'cause I keep my mind occupied with other less hurtful things like family, friends, road trips, leftovers, hangovers, Netflix binges, typewriters, heartache, whiskey, poetic clichés along with the reality of me miles ahead from the perception everyone has, the tired face I show the world 'cause I'm tough, 'cause I won't allow you to be the end of me, 'cause even if I love you a little bit more with the years even though I miss you a little bit less, that's a victory I'd like to claim, something that you can't take away me from, 'cause despite what you've heard, there's life after death after all.

My Favorite

I guess you've always been my favorite. So please, please understand that if I'm mute, if I seem distant, if I walk away while you approach, it's because eye contact would slay me. I love you because I can't have you and I can't have you because I love you. The air is suffocating when we're not sharing it, and yet I don't want you near. The mere sight of your lips moving, making way for a perfectly knit smile, kills me, every time. And if you log on to Instagram and read this piece, please don't question me about it. You should know by now that I'm a coward first, a lover second, a poet third, and you're my favorite, and you know this, and always will be even if we never are. And that is that.

Be Good, Josh!

I'd tell him to be good, to please stay still for a few precious seconds, to stare at the carousel of cartoonish creatures circling above his tiny bitty head, and to let me sleep a bit instead, but he just laughs. I'd beg him to work with me here, to let me doze off for an hour or two, because it's 3AM and Daddy needs some semblance of sleep, but he looks at me like I'm crazy and just laughs. He goo's and gah's, he smiles, his eyes light up, he cries a little, he cries a ton, and then he laughs. And I've already exhausted Cartoon Network's schedule, and I'd still try to reason with him. "Mommy's been at the hospital all night wiping old people's asses, and she's gonna do yours in just a matter of time!" Then I remember that if I don't take care of your stinky poo, you might get a rash too, but he does not care and just laughs and laughs all the way to 7AM, just in time for Mommy to get home. Daddy has to go work and baby finally goes to bed.

Another Love Letter to Love

I guess this will be my love letter to you. New loves unable to accept past loves and past loves unable to accept new ones. Because yeah, I've loved before, and will continue to do so – shocking I know. And I've loved hard, and I've written them love poems, just like the ones I've written you but different, for it's the way I learned to express myself ever since I was a child. And yes, I tend to do the same romantic gestures because my personality is impersonal. Feelings do tend to grow accustomed to the new love as a person, and I'll never try to reinvent the wheel installed within me. It'll just keep spinning and hovering over insecure waters. It'll continue to love a million times over until it stops with the woman engineered for me, with no excuses nor pretexts to stop us. So, this is my love letter to you, and I promise to love you as much as I've loved before, if I can only get 100% or more in return instead of the 50% you keep giving me, love poems and all.

Atlantic Philly/Miami City

Shit! Here we fucking go. Get out of work at 4, drive to the carwash, make sure the piece of junk sparkles and smells nice, get a bottle of wine, go home, get ready, drink 2 beers, get your hookah on, head out to Philly, pick her up at the airport, park somewhere that's convenient, try not to plow over people, arrive at her gate, make sure to kiss her well between smiles, head to a mutual friend's house, drink the night away, get up early, wreck a thrift store, vinyls, typewriters, books, cool vintage stuff, pick up another friend at a bus stop, smoke, drink, write poetry, sing songs, let's go, head to A.C the next day, fun at the beach, more drinks, WWE event, LOL Cena wins, Atlantic Palace crowned us king and queen, overlooking the ocean, under the boardwalk, over the moon, swoon, love, Garden's Basin, steak sandwiches and juicy burgers for lunch docked at the bay, head back to Philly, barhop with friends, dark and delicious craft brews, get to the airport, a sweet kiss goodbye to hold me up until next time, say goodbye forever gypsy love, drive back home.

Spoonful of Loving

Spread your curls on the bedspread like butter on toast, like Amazonian vines suffocating our bedroom. I'm digging deep into your big brown eyes under the constellations, with the intention to camp there for a while, planting my flag on your beauty mark before ever second-guessing and wondering how the fuck I ever got so lucky. I'd take a closer look at the full moon masquerading as your lips and prepare to land on soft terrain loaded with kisses ready to satisfy my hunger and feed my appetite. Soon, spoonfuls of loving are to follow, shoved in my mouth whilst my thumb's logged on yours, sucking and licking on your tongue as the log catches fire from our bodies ablaze, and there goes the fireplace along with the damned movie date we never intended on watching any fucking way, on another long forgotten winter night dedicated to carnal worship, melting down to ashes.

Bear Mountain Beauty

Is that normal? Is it even possible? Is that even allowed? Charlie and I looked at each other in disbelief then looked back at her, the most beautiful specimen our eyes had ever seen at the time. But wait until I begin to describe her for you guys! It was difficult to find the words then, when she walked by, leaving us bumbling like a couple of fools, like a pair of creeps staring at her, frozen in time, but we knew those adjectives were there, stuck in our throats making a knot only a gaze from her extraterrestrial eyes could untie, but she didn't offer one. It's almost as if she was glowing in the Bear Mountain altitude, wearing a force field separating her from the multitude that had gathered for Oktoberfest, beer mug in hand. It's almost like she was there and she wasn't. She wore one of those big hats of Victorian times. She was a throwback to when beauties were immortalized in daguerreotypes of One Hundred Years of Solitude folklore, a Remedios the Beauty ripped out of extraordinary tales and personified for all of us to see, the crowds, snowy trees, and damp clouds, Charlie and I astounded. But wait until I begin to describe her for you guys, any moment now, soon as the words come to me, if they ever do.

And That's How She Slays

And that's how she slays. It's almost like she decided to motherfuck conventional wisdom from an early age and forwent the delusions of little girls of all ages striving for perfection. She just doesn't care. And that's how she slays, just standing there, telling me all about her latest night of debauchery, relating them in the most whimsical manner. It's like she's smiling the whole time she's talking, almost simultaneously, the only one in on the joke. And that's how she slays, when she suddenly stops, realizing she's not hungover but still drunk. It's almost like she's hitting above average if you count the times she bats her eyelashes to bring my bench-warming heart to its knees. And that's how she slays. And that's how she slays me. And she fucking knows it. That bitch.

Butterflied Stomach

How could it be? She butterflies me some kisses and meticulously plants them in the pit of my stomach, making me come back for more, to watch 'em flutter out of my mouth and into hers, to see them roll back into a cocoon when she walks away leaving my eager lips aching for more. There's no Chapstick I'd rather wear than her mouth on mine. There's no warmth I'd rather have in the blistering cold. There's no scarf I'd rather use than her arms around my neck. There's no smile I'd rather wake up to in the middle of a furious blizzard on this side of hell, barely missing heaven, to melt the snow accumulated much to Satan's chagrin and blow up my laughs when I deflate, when I try and fail to convince her to stay a wee bit longer, when I'm out of reasons to guilt her conscience into staying, when dawn tells us it's time to go, when there's no woman I'd rather touch, breathe, or smoke than her scorching kiss wedged in-between our fire in the coldest of winters.

Chocolate Girl of Grapefruit Lips

Tequila turned out to be our saving grace, chocolate girl with the grapefruit lips. We agreed on a double date even though we didn't like each other much. But our friends needed to get laid and so we showcased our selfless natures. It was like a scene out of Goodfellas. Tommy and Henry would be proud. They snuck away to take care of their urges while we engaged in awkward conversation along with that treacherous tequila smiling its evil Mexican teeth in approval. We shared some shots, wedged a lime between our laughter, went on to drink sloppy kisses after. Chalk another W for our dear friend Cuervo. Our bodies were the sore winners the morning after.

Once Upon a Pig

She was sweet to me and I cheated like a dumbass. She found out through a tagged picture on Facebook, of all fucking things. I left her for another only to come back a month later, begging for forgiveness after I realized my douchey mistake. She stood by the door and wouldn't let me in, even though I had a pretty-ass bouquet in one hand, my heart in the other. She started listing the reasons why we couldn't be together, trust being the main one, with tears streaming down her face. Her heartbreak broke me. I could no longer resist and so I grabbed her, threw her against the wall and forcefully kissed her neck, mouth, forehead, nose, until she eventually caved. We ended up on the living room floor making angry hate-infused love on her part, desperately trying to hold on, on mine, and then she coldly said, "Get off, you can't stay the night. I want you to leave and never come back. Please, just go." I was deflated and lost, but as destiny would have it, the moment I stepped out of her door I was greeted by a text message reading, "Hey boy, I'm coming over to do laundry ;) See you soon!" And so life went on to live another day, handing me another story to tell, briefly.

You Looked So F'N Pretty Today...

You looked so pretty today and how could you? I've long been disarmed by your smile, sitting across a phone screen or in person, thinking about the things we'll never be while daydreaming about the possibilities of being with you. So why in the fuck would you look so damn good today? You're not doing me any favors. I have to furiously bite my fist as you walk by and all I can do is reach for paper and pen to capture the moment and post it on IG later, hoping you'd give me a read and a like for my efforts, a wink and a nudge in compliance because you know better. You're my sinking ship, the spitting image of Queen Anne Boleyn, the breathing illusion I can't grasp even when you're talking, wondering why I always look so angry, trying to hang your mischievous Harley Quinn grin on my face. So tell me, how dare you look this fucking good today? And go about our conversation nonchalant, knowing damn well that I'm dying inside to take our bodies on a drinking binge, dig our toes on the Atlantic City sand and kiss, take the moment our lips drift apart to stare and think, who the fuck ever knew we would look this damn good together?

Twice Upon a Time in Mexico

She worshipped the ground I walked on
in the hedonistic Aztec tradition. She was sweeter
than Mezcal after the agave loses its sting. Blame
the thieved kissed she refused to surrender.
Single mom living in a 1-bedroom shack, chief of
my cuisine, chef of atomic spice souring up my
brow. We built shrines in the living room to get
intoxicated, performed full-bodied rituals and
watched movies, racing frantically along the Slum
Dog Millionaires of the world while her child
slept. Maybe I should've sewn my nomadic skin
into hers, but my young and thirsty tongue still
had some more soulless fucking to do. If anything,
no woman who followed was able to lace her
Chucks or love me senseless like she could.

Rewriting the Cold War

Ever heard of the Cuban Missile Crisis? The Bay of Pigs? Well, the aforementioned communist Caribbean nation had Russian missiles at its disposal, firmly pointed at the U.S, creating tension, paranoia, and instability. Now, I want us to do something radically different. I want you to launch yourself at me. I want you to hit me with everything you got. Let's not worry about the irreparable consequences that might follow, and show them how history should've played out.

Pink Hoodie

She thought it'd be a good idea to pack the memories made in 3 short months in a 4x6 box before going back to Australia and leaving me on the hook for another year. The contents of the shoebox as I recall: pictures of our first date frolicking all over Times Square, the fun night she dressed up as a school girl, tied me to a chair, and fed me straight Jean Bean to the tune of 50 Cent's "In Da Club." Also included was our 6oz "Love Jar" stuffed with love letters, movie ticket stubs, and Australian currency to go along with banal promises of forever. But the coup de grace was that damn pink sweatshirt preserving her perfume. I'd take it out and lay it down to sleep next to me through the winter. The image of her disappearing into the airport didn't hurt as long as the sweatshirt kept the mirage of her company intact. Years later, I was in a relationship again and I asked my buddy Matt to dispose of the box on his way upstate. He told me he threw it in the ocean, and that the waves drowned our pictures down under –how fitting – but little did I know Matt had lied, and a few years later he returned with the box and that damn pink sweatshirt still breathing, still sweating, looking to camouflage her solitude in the other side of the world, followed by a remorseful phone call 5 years in the making saying "I should've never left you."

Fight of the Century

'Twas the fight of the century! Two caged fighters about to throw down, the gloves were off, venomous tongues lacking fucks to give, lashing insults, whipping until bleeding. She confessed to her cheating ways, yet my own discrepancies stayed tightlipped. She packed her shit, tears were shed, she flung copies of her keys at my head and off to Mom's she went, leaving the door ajar enough for solitude to creep in the minute she walked out. Then the days turned into weeks, the weeks into months, and still she wouldn't return despite my emphatic pleads and pathetic phone calls. I refused to lock the front door just in case she'd have a sudden change of heart and come back sleepwalking on a sleepless night to lay her head next to mine, on her side of the bed I had kept intact since she left. And when she finally did, I had started wearing a new love, and when she texted that she was right outside, the door had already been shut and I could no longer let her in, even if she would've kept the keys, like I always wanted.

Doing Her Dirty Laundry

And here you are, knocking on my door, ready to do laundry sans the dirty clothes and detergent, clinging to the fledging integrity of your husband shoved up your cunt. You were mine now, and those empty lips craving to be filled with every inch I had to offer were about to go mute, alongside heavy kisses like a torrential downpour, touching and fucking like Armageddon was here. There were some things you would forbid and that was okay, because it was the way you kept some of you to yourself, and whatever was left reserved for him, whenever you gave me an hour of passion, stretching 60 ungodly minutes on the Trojan you gleefully mounted, to feel fulfilled with the one guy who loved you to pieces and gave you dick for days in an hour. You used to jet down the parkway, the journey getting longer the closer you'd come, to see me and my puppy eyes that wouldn't accept the role of a side piece, but had to put up with, until the day I no longer took your calls, the very same day you finally decided to leave him and I had already moved on, only to find you again clothed in misery many years later, without a man to call home.

Maybe the One

And maybe then you'll be the one to stop me on my tracks before the urgency of a mid-life crisis creeps in, as you most likely already know if you're the one meant to be, 'cause I've always been the one to run in slow motion ever since I was glued to the TV as a kid, watching the former Pamela Lee safeguarding my dreams in a red swimsuit, sunny hair, and bright lips, taking off without a hurry, while not understanding what the hell was going on in my pants, and maybe then you'll be the one hiding in plain sight, like a cruel game of peek-a-boo, sipping on IPA hops, hoping to spot you across the room, playing a risky game of hopscotch toward each other, a half-hop at a time, pausing the space time continuum, breaking the 4th wall, interlocking eyes, kissing without touching, as the music flows its natural course but only we can hear it, with heartbeats pounding 10 seconds apart like that scene in Tim Burton's film Big Fish, like contractions on the way to the hospital on a crazy night, 'cause maybe, just maybe you'll be the one crazy enough to make me a daddy again, and gift us a daughter with pinchable cheeks and an even bigger smile, plunging our sky into eternal sunshine, spotless minds, maybe then, you'll be the one.

Gypsy Eyes

Almond-shaped and light brown, weary of the souls they've consumed during her lifetime, I'm a reflection of them. That's where my love affair began. I loved how her eyes hung on to every word my eyes spoke like a child trying to register a new language, how they'd sit still intensely across from mine as we made love in a pool of desire, in her mind's eye my eyes could do no wrong, her eyes sagged with love and her pupils dilated when I put it in, delighted in my grace, gazes locked in and engraved. Her eyes belonged to me then, because they long deserted her face the moment I decided to wear them. In her eyes I was a god, chiseled out of marble and stone no matter how many times I fucked up, beer belly and all. Now her eyes are gone, packed their bags never to be heard from again, grown tired of my shit and wandered away, because gypsy eyes know how to say goodbye when the time comes, and they never look back.

Of Love & Other Dirty Business

Round 2:

The Collateral of a Failed Relationship

Twitchy

I remember that one week your eye wouldn't stop twitching. It had you freaking out and complaining to the high heavens. And then, you'd Google the symptoms. "Why is my eye twitching?" That thing looked like it had a life of its own! You'd look at me and say, "Babe! Is my eye still twitching?" with a lovable and frustrated frown on your face, pointing scared at the left one. I'd blow on it and kiss it, and tell you it's from stress and lack of sleep. I'd remind you that you're not Wonder Woman or Supergirl, and that in fact, mortality was your guise. I'd plead with you to stop worrying so much about things beyond your control, that the world's problems were not all yours to handle. And now, I sit in my car on a breezy autumn day, hands crossed on top of the wheel like yours used to, my left eye starts to twitch and I wonder if it's you trying to communicate from the afterlife, if there happened to be any after us.

6Av Blues

6Av blues still lingers, fresh off a tour on the 7 train, lost in Queens, NY. We emerged in the lower east's jazz lounge somehow. You had the buttermilk chicken with cornbread, I had the roasted salmon with mash while the band played Whiplash and we got drunk with laughter. It was nothing but gravy back then, Poets Café, Central Park West, paying our respects to the slain Lennon, kicking it groovy with Strawberry Field's mayor, followed by love and rainbows adorning our skyline. Then the conversation shifted to renting a sports car we had no intention of driving in real life. We would take it down to the Florida Keys and get a suite in that curious hotel with all the rooms named after famous writers. Hemingway looked good offering a Caribbean view, but we settled on Emily instead – soft, posh, quaint. Writers contrasting our personalities, ghastly versions of ourselves taking notes of their living doppelgängers trying to make a precarious life viable. Now here I am, a few broken years later, driving down the Keys in an overpriced sports car I had no intention of ever renting, alone.

The Jig is up

I guess we all know when the jig is up. About a month before the final curtain call I spent a month nestled on the couch, part of the cold war we waged, neither giving up an inch, dying in no man's land. I, stupidly waited for her to come downstairs and get me in the middle of the night and ask me back to bed, but she never did. I'd cook up a truce disguised as breakfast to get back in her good graces, yet dinner no longer waited for me when I got back home after a long shift. Some nights I tried to crawl back into bed while she slept, only to be greeted by the cold of her back and the warmth of her indifference. She was now from Russia with hate, and her precarious ship had long sailed to other shores, leaving me stranded. I guess we all know when the jig is up, and now my bags are packed and by the door, patiently waiting to be delivered into uncertainty.

The End of Ends

And then, at the end of ends, you remember the last of everything – the last lovemaking session, the last few smiles shared, the last restaurant you went to, the last fight, the last movie you watched, the last kiss, the last walk on the beach, the last civilized conversation, the final argument, doors slammed, the nail in the coffin, the coffin in the nail, and at the very last you remember to ask, whatever happened to your best friend the moment you became strangers?

Kissing In-Between Kissing

Truth is, we were always kissing. It was like a hobby of ours, a blood sport to say the least. Something to do on long afternoons when we couldn't stand the sight of each other. We'd kiss the fade off polaroids. We'd kiss during Sandra Bullock movie marathons. We'd kiss first thing in the morning before reaching for a toothbrush, before and after meals, because we didn't know what else to do with ourselves and the thought of our lips being made for anything else sounded ridiculous. And so we kissed and kissed, we even kissed in-between kisses and carried each other's taste for weeks on end. Kissing became the glue holding us together long after our expiration date, when our mouths ran dry and the wealth of kisses once given could no longer be replenished.

On Wasted Time

And then she tossed my bags out the doors and told me to go waste someone else's time, and off I went. And then she told me to go fuck myself and find someone else's time to waste, and that I did. And then she told me to up and die and go waste someone else's time, and I was dead. Then I found her while time was wasting, she cradled my head on her lap, putting my restless and homeless spirit to sleep saying, "Thank you, thank you for wasting all of your time on me."

Things We Liked

Amongst the things we liked, amongst the things we shared, were a sweet tooth for adventure, a toothbrush when I forgot mine, Motown, Marvin, Stevie, Al Green, The Jackson 5, the New Edition of old school hip-hop driving me out of my mind and straight into her. We'd ambush quiet little towns, marvel at quaint antiques, colored houses by the river banks penciled-in along with the open road closing, forgetting the miles traveled and the things we no longer share and no longer like, because we no longer are who we used to be, amongst other things.

Sunday Morning Breakfast

Sunday mornings, waking up miles apart after cuddling the night to bed. Our maple bodies find each other hapless, magnetically coming together, synchronizing, falling into place like Lego blocks, and that's when love became breakfast, leftover kisses for lunch. I'd go down to the kitchen and make your favorite eggs and toast with a bit of butter. I bring back some O.J. and those giddy eyes making way for a joyous smile would light up. We'd turn on the TV and watch House Hunters, imagining a dream life through a screen, watch History Channel documentaries, catch up on our favorite shows before embedding the afternoon into our skin, gracing full lips to sleep, fingers intertwined and locked. Needless to say, the brisk breeze of autumn whisking me awake already knows, Sunday mornings just ain't the same without you.

Handsome, Sexy Man

She always made it a habit to make me feel good no matter what self-loathing shitty job I was holding. She'd say, "You look kinda sexy in that uniform, can you wear it to bed?" She'd transform a smile from a grouchy mug with her moonlight, every time. "My handsome, sexy man, dinner will be ready when you get home. Don't keep me waiting, you know how to wake me up ;)" She'd sext teasing selfies chock-full of x's and o's. I'd eat countless of red lights to rush in and rub the lipstick off her lips and plunge. On snowy nights like these I can still hear her kissable voice, having good conversations with her new handsome, sexy man in my honor, over dinner.

The Final Stop

This... this is a reality now. This is really happening. I go in the house for the final time and start to pack my things. I grab my Oktoberfest mug outta the Freezer, clothes outta the closet, my books outta the shelf leaving you the ones I've given you – Junot's "This is How You Lose Her" and something else by TD Jakes. I stop for a long minute to contemplate our picture still sitting pretty above the fireplace, the one taken in the nosebleed seats of that Red Sox/Phillies game of our honeymooned summer. I run my fingers across your face and kiss it. Yeah I know, kinda cheesy, kinda pathetic, and "Something" by The Beatles starts playing in my head on an endless loop. I run upstairs, make my way to the attic and dust off the very same typewriter in which I'm writing this piece on, then I come to the realization of one fucked up thing – there's nothing crueler in life than leaving someone you love because it's the right thing to do, for both, for growth, for peace, even if you're leaving with none, even if you're escaping into the vast prison of a newfound freedom, just in time for winter.

Breaking up, Breaking Down

We broke up so many times people kept expecting us to get back together at any moment. "So, are you guys back together yet?" And when I'd say no, they'd give me this puzzled look. I'd tell them that this time it's sticking and it's for good and they'd dismiss my claims with a "Nah, ya'll will get back together soon, you'll see!" And they'd walk away feeling like it was just a matter of time before we did. And even though it's been two years since I last talked to you and there's a good chance we'll never see each other again, our lives are forever linked and intertwined in the tongues of people who think we still love each other, in the hearts of souls of who may or may not know better than us.

Plight of the Coward

And then you hurt me, and I retaliated by doing the most cowardly thing possible – I hurt you as well. That wasn't enough though, I took it one step further. I destroyed you from the inside. I destroyed any future relationship you might've had after I left instead of walking away with dignity and the pain of knowing you've killed me too many times over to know the difference. But that's not how cowards operate, fuck no. They never stop scheming, or writing flimsy excuses like this one to make themselves feel better, like the shit we put ourselves through, sticking around long past our expiration date, trying to save something that just didn't work, like a couple of cowards not knowing when or how to give it up, and so they keep on fighting until the end.

The Poems I Still Write

Just when I think I've run out of love poems to write I think of you. I think of you forgetting me. I think of you forgetting to love me when I needed you. I think of you forgetting to love me when I needed you to remember the love poems I still write when I think of you.

14th St...Back for Me

And then she came back for me like a scene out of those classic black and white films from the 40's. She ran down the 14th St train station's steps and caught up to my soles before I got on the path. "Would you go back to Atlantic City with me?" she asked, drawing a smile from my face, kissing me a kiss, as the locomotive's whistle blew past and I nodded a relieved "yes" in agreement, losing ourselves in the commute's commotion, marking it the last time love found a way to stop us in our tracks, before disappearing between us, forever.

3,722 Emails and None of Them Yours

Shot you an email years ago, the last of our conversations, the culmination of a week-long struggle trying to get closure through digital correspondence that'd put carrier pigeons to shame and smoke signals disguised as clouds to dust. We agreed on everything that didn't work, expressed sorrow for the things that did, followed by regrets of what could've been if we had kept our emotions in check. Now years have gone by along with women, alcohol, late nights, and nothing's changed on my part, and still I don't know a damned thing about you, which is why I keep my eye on the dusty inbox, 3,722 emails, half unopened, most of them junk, hoping that one day you'll remember that I still exist, hoping the next time my phone goes off that hopefully it's you.

Because I Still

Because I still piss in the tub when I have a hard-on. Because I still have your angry text messages and loving voicemails saved. Because I still drink myself into a coma when you're not looking, dead when you are. Because I still need to incorporate fruits into my diet, hard apple cider not included. Because my frail ego is still in love with the sound of my own voice, because no one else likes to hear me talking. Because my ghost is still in the backyard writing away the afternoon – seriously though, tell him to drop that shit and get dinner started. Because I still refuse to shower in the morning. Because I still despise all of your favorite TV Evangelist/con artists. Because I still hit on anything that breathes only to feel wanted, even if I have no intention of ever chasing or caring. Because I still haven't changed a bit and I'm still a mess, and dirty clothes pile up everywhere except the laundry basket. Because I still use inappropriate language whenever I see fit – fuck, cunt, motherfucker, shit, piss. Because I'm still infatuated with the leftover taste of your addictive lips. Because I still rummage for your essence after 3AM when it cruelly breezes by my nose. Because I still can't figure out how to live, and let go.

Space Oddity

Driving into the void – oblivion, darkness, and all the space in the world plotting to consume me – piloting my spaceship on lifeless pavement. I float, I cringe, I daydream, I just don't feel a thing, after getting off that eternal night shift that kept my soul and sent me en route to the turmoil and solace found on a bed beside a woman that far and long ago stopped giving a fuck about me. I was now a space oddity beneath the stars and over the moon, looking to land on deserted arms, justifying a reason to stay another day as Bowie's "Ground Control to Major Tom" replayed over and over again on a 20 minute drive, signaling emptiness at every red light trying to block my way home, to pull up and tip toe up the stairs, and crawl into bed facing the glacier of her back, avoiding to start another war that'll never find an end, until the day I finally built up the courage to strap on a jetpack, point my cursor at the sky and shoot my ass into infinity, and from a distance be able to wave goodbye, this time for good.

Trading Numbers

And so we decided to start talking, trading numbers and texting throughout the day, beginning a friendship and graduating to phone calls, subsequently dating, followed by sex 20 times a day, 20 more at night, and then we moved in together, went ahead and started a family, made plans to grow old while remaining young at heart with the cliché mantra – live, love, laugh. But some things in life aren't meant to last once routine sinks in and feelings dissipate, getting replaced by hate and discordance. And here I am missing you, but too stubborn to call. And there you are, loving me but too hardheaded to admit defeat. And so we're back again at the start, like two strangers before we met, like we never happened and never dared to trade phone numbers in the first place.

All We'll Have is Pictures

And when the sons of daughters we never had ask, this is how I'll summarize our lifetime together: in pictures. Facebook albums brimmed with pictures, computer folders stuffed with pictures, shoe boxes full of pictures, Instagram timelines sick of pictures, iPhones, iClouds, handbags, wallets, calculator apps in disguise hiding our naughty sides, well you get the picture. And once I found out that deceitful camera loved you more than I did, I wanted to smash the fucker against the wall and switch to videos because I know how much you hated those fucking things, crushed under the weight of nearly 1,000 pictures of a happy us, 4 years' worth of smiles abandoned, erased and decomposed with just a click of the mouse.

As It Turns Out...

And as it turns out, everyone happens to run into you and then you ask, "How's the fam? How are things?" How's everyone except for me. I'm a taboo subject of your thoughts, persona non grata of your lips, even when people ask if you've seen me around, and even though we share the same small city and big town, we manage to keep away someway, somehow. Maybe it's that internal GPS running us separate ways, maybe it's the fact that we still know each other's routines and which places to avoid on a specific time of day, only for you to run into my family instead and ask again, "How are things?" How's life, how's the moon, the stars and even the fucking sky? How's everyone with the exception of me. Now you tell me, forgetful lover, how are you without?

Wedding Crashers

We'd crash weddings like a sporting event, a hunger game of sorts, something to bury in our psyche, front and center of our minds, 'cause the thought of a possible wedding kept the fights at bay and reminded us of our end goal, but I'll get to that in a bit. Weddings – you went for the pageantry, the love, the romance, and witnessing not a single dry eye in the room including yours, and how you'd steal the show with your stunning dress, such a gorgeous specimen by my hand, I bet plenty of those grooms knew they were making a mistake as soon as they laid eyes on you. Meanwhile, I went for the camaraderie, the drunkenness, the showing you off in one hand and the entire open bar in the other, the fun, the seeing you happy 'cause in the back of your mind there was a small girl dreaming of a day like this, thinking of the Pinterest wedding dress you had repinned, and how we'd be ready to take the plunge soon enough. We got married so many times in a 4-year span. We flew from the backyard on a cold summer night to a warm Caribbean beach, sand in our toes, I wore Bermuda shorts, Habanera shirt and sandals, you wore the beautiful in and out to go with a crown of flowers, ready to unload the world's greatest kiss at the sound of an "I do." We daydreamed across Europe, we even got hitched in Brazil, but by the time we woke up we no longer cared about us, yet we still attended weddings, but forgot to crash our own.

A Very Bohemian Christmas

I'm finally home for the holidays; it's been a long time coming. The years had accumulated inches high while I kept my distance, but now, I was finally here, tracing my steps in the snow, from the car to the front door where a jubilant little girl awaited, ready to wrap her arms around my waist. I see presents hugging the tree, my girl's under the mistletoe, smiling, waiting for a kiss, gift in hand, love on her face. A warm meal greets me at the table, my little boy's excited to see me happy as all hell, glad that I finally made it back. I tell them the story of my precarious journey. They sit around me like a campfire, attentively listening to Daddy speak. And that's when they start disappearing, one by one, before I can finish, along with the presents, the lights, and the tree, then I hear the door slamming shut and that's when I realize that I'm home alone, and not a creature was stirring for Christmas.

It's Been A Minute Since Forever Ago

It's been a minute since forever ago, the last time I've seen you, turning your back, closing up shop to what it once was, dreams notwithstanding, waving goodbye from the heart's memory, your new home away from me, from us. It's been a minute since forever ago. I still see your old Honda around town, same model, year, and color, scratched to all hell, only to be usurped by someone else at the wheel. I could've sworn it was you, even if it's been a minute since. I still feel your love at the pit of my stomach at the prospect of seeing you again if only for a brief moment, and then I wonder if you've changed, straightened your hair, gained or lost weight, grew the inner beauty to match your physical demands, learned how to channel the strength to avoid settling for souls who do not reflect you in any way or shape, if you managed to learn lessons in my mistakes, finding comfort in solitude just as I pretend to, even if it kills you, like it killed me, if you figured out how to relearn how to kiss since the last time I did, because I need you to teach me how to teach you to forget me, us.

Going Back Home

I guess you've known this for quite some time now – she's sitting at home patiently waiting, whether you're in your cubicle impatiently staring at the clock, writing wistful notes for your own amusement to kill a time that won't stay dead for long and moves at a turtle's pace, or somewhere in the stock room of a conglomerate giant feeding you minimum wage when love is the one nutrient you're craving. You do know that once those 8 hours are up she'll still be waiting, doesn't matter if it's been dog days, a few insufferable months, or lightyears spent wandering the outside edges of outer space, squandering chances, trying to hitchhike a comet for a return trip to the galaxy of her kitchen, where she'll be marinating a kiss for hours, months, and years in the making, ripe for the young age of old souls who wisely avoid clueless clichés telling us that there are other fish in the sea when no one swims as good as her, biding her time, slow cooking everything you've earned to perfection next to the stove, hair tied up in a bun, wearing an apron, and fixing your favorite dish, just in time for you to come and knock on the door along with the biggest smile she's ever seen, saying "Babe, I'm home, and I missed you."

Happenstance by The Pool

And then it was you, the kids, and the dog, happenstance on a beautiful sunny day by the pool, a sharp contrast to the ugly muck sitting outside my window when it rains. I can't help it, the gloom and doom the clouds threatens us with helps me write pretty things, like that one glorious afternoon I'm sure you still remember, reclined comfortably on your beach chair with your aviator sunglasses on, green and yellow towel and matching two-piece swimming suit. The kids were engaging in lethal water warfare, veering off to the deep end every time we took our eyes from them to concentrate on our own. Happy was going bat-shit insane at the sight of all the squirrels rummaging the area, he was hyped as all fuck. And then, there was me, giddily collecting the precious memories the day kept gifting so I could write about them years later. Then, I pointed my phone's camera on her and asked "How much do you love me, my love?" To which she replied "I love you deeper than the ocean, babe," as I zoomed in on her ridiculously perfect lips to fully capture every word that came out of them, because I wanted to believe. But the kids are no longer here, and Happy has passed on since, and while the ocean still sits there, the love we once shared floats aimlessly along, alive and dead, casually dipping and coming up for air, a castaway in my writing.

Goodnight, Babe

I found her at our old place looking for me, under the pillow, in-between the sofa cushions, in the fridge. "I'm here, babe," I let her know from the bedroom door. She then set her eyes on me, waiting to hear something else and I gave it to her. "I miss you and I love you." She hugged me tight and broke into tears. "I'm sorry, I'm sorry, babe," she repeated. " I needed to hear those words from you." I calmed her down, held her face. "Do you want to see that movie later? The one you like with Tyler Perry?" She nodded in approval, wiping her tears and smiling in compliance. "Okay, babe, I'll get it from Red Box." She kissed me for the final time and walked away. I woke up to her spirit deserting my body never to return. After years of silence, this is as good a closure that I'm ever going to get. The only way it could happen – in dreams. Goodnight, babe. I'll miss you.

Of Love & Other Dirty Business

Love. How to describe it? It's the only life occurrence on this side of death that we can't grasp or understand, because it arrives at a moment's notice and leaves without packing its bags. To comprehend love is to decipher the dead sea scrolls without any knowledge of ancient tongues. To fully get it, it's the equivalent of believing in Santa Clause and colored bunnies that shit chocolate. Love wraps you around its heart's pinky, convinces you that every song played on the radio is about you and your very special relationship. It meticulously places dragonflies at the pit of your belly. And then, after all the sickening pageantry and goodness, earthshaking sex, and soon-to-be unfulfilled promises, it snatches the flying carpet from beneath you, leaving you empty after eating everything you had to offer without footing the bill. Now time passes, so we mourn and eulogize it, we keep it nice and pristine in the heart's memory, then we remember it's still breathing, so we exhume it, drink it on the rocks or straight. We let it chaperone our solitude on long lost nights when we have nothing else to live for. And so we die again in its name, only to resurrect it in the morning, pretending to be okay and determined to face life armed with a slingshot and a few meager pellets like the ghetto version of Cupid. But now it's different, or so we think. Maybe a little wiser, maybe a little more stupid, but still 100% dumbfounded by its power and uncanny ability to change the course of our lives.

Hemingway once wrote, "Write the truest sentence you know," and here's mine: Love and death are interchangeable because they both leave the same lasting effect after it's over. In other words, you cease to exist.

Of Love & Other Dirty Business

Round 3:

Of Other Dirty Business

The Drunk Poet Drives

Sigh, here we fucking go. Leave for the club by 10PM to see your friend Tasha perform, promise yourself you'll leave right after, end up leaving at 4, pass out drunk, roll out of bed at 7, drink a beer, jump in the car without a change of clothes, reeking of booze, lipstick, and hangovers, drive 8 hours to Providence, RI for a book fair, show 'em your stuff, get on the mic, kill it, get off, pose for pictures with the 3 people you managed to wow, sell 5 copies, leave and go back to your car, find a liquor store, buy a Lime-a-Rita, drive 2 more hours to Lawrence, MA, to see Grandma, she's surprised to see you, party with the fam until 3AM, get up at 10, kill a 12-pack with the cousin, get on the Mass turnpike by 2, get home by 9PM, drink more beer, go the fuck to sleep, wait, hold the phone, the Atlantic City nightlife is calling, leave the house by 12.

Atlantic City Part 1

Here I hold a map of the Atlantic City area and its neighboring towns, where every corner is saturated by a memory of an ex, a current, a future. The inlet where Hurricane Sandy displaced us for a few days. The bay by the Garden Basin where we usually made love without protection. Ventnor City and its winds tossing our newly developed pictures down the street. The shore atop a lifeguard's nest, home of many first kisses followed by seconds and thirds. Our last apartment in Margate before our relationship met the unforgiving guillotine. Galloway Twp, riddled with explosives at every turn of the wheel. That Mexican restaurant with the best nachos this continent has ever seen, Mexico included. And there you are still, and here I am always, putting the pieces together of everything that could've been but never was. Joaquin Sabina wrote that there's no worst nostalgia than longing for the things that never came to be, and ironically, no good writing is able to exist without them either.

My 25th Hour

You there! You know who you are, you know where you're going, but you're still trying to figure out how to get there and that's okay. You never learned how to settle, so please, please understand this: People like you, Ottis. Wherever you land you'll make new friends, get into new adventures, possibly meet a new heart to slay or two, maybe write a few more books, and quite possibly, maybe if you're lucky, sleep more than six hours a day. Imagine that? Six fucking hours! So, just get behind the wheel and drive, and remember that no matter how many exits you may miss along the way, life will still be there, waiting.

1950s America

We usually walk away in opposite directions only to find ourselves in the same place, sharing the same nostalgia and slice of Americana the open road brings. Somewhere in the Midwest, there are stories yet to be told, hidden in the remnants of diners long abandoned, surviving entities of decades gone by. The decayed spirit of the 50's still intact – malt shops and jukeboxes living up the mood, happy days and rock 'n roll before Vietnam. You can feel the ghost of Buddy Holly haunting these walls and a weeping Richie Valenzuela remorseful to have boarded that plane. This is where we meet, her and I, sitting across each other, conversing with our eyes and looking around for tales to devour, for sweeping stories that'll never see the light of dawn until we hit the open road again and nostalgia finally succumbs at the end of this sentence.

Thankful for Abandoned Airports

People come and go. I see them descending on my heart's landing strip, knowing full well that it's only the idea of time keeping them here, like forgotten luggage in abandoned airports, which is why I am thankful. Thankful for those who stay long after I broke their wings, swallowed and cancelled their return trips to feed my needs and fearful ego. Thankful of the people willing to share a love without merit, without conditions, people who could care less about the fine print. Thankful of sightless lovers, givers of forehead kisses, and lenders of heart emojis when you need them most. Thankful for friendships all over the world, sending hugs via carrier pigeons, high on liquor, drunk on coke. Writers equally lonely and fucked, but still breathing, still feeling, still dying. Thankful for the love of my life, every time I meet her just to watch her go. She keeps me writing much to my chagrin, 'cause I'm such an ungrateful prick. And for that, I'm thankful.

I Don't Care About Things When I do

I don't care about this old Sprint LG phone holding pictures hostage of an ex that found my comics collection to be childish and immature. Fuck no. I ain't about to throw away Gambit & Rogue for a relationship. I don't care if you don't support my selfie as long as you support my writing, and speaking of, I don't care about the multi-layered pictures you post for show. Nowadays you gotta go a few filters deep to really get to know people. I don't care about your lunch or dinner, and neither does the rest of the world. Feel free to choke on it. I don't care about your resting bitch face when I'm trying to start a conversation for fuck's sake. I have an Instagram account and a shit-ton of followers that'll help me ignore you at a whim. No, I do not care about petty, worthless things, but Imma still write about them, because it's what the fuck I do. Sadly.

95 South in the Way of Thanksgiving

Here you fucking go. Get outta work by 5, go to your aunt's house, shower, change clothes, steal some cake from your cousin's baby shower the night before, stop by the liquor store for some happy juice, get gas from Wawa and ignore the crackhead trying to hitch a ride to Baltimore, head up to I-95 and take a dive south, look for a rock station to get the Led out, drive through a billion tolls in Delaware, find yourself in a stadium parking lot somewhere in Maryland taking a piss – fuck the Redskins – destroy about 4 cans of Monsters before sleep creeps in, keep going into the heart of Virginia, the Carolinas, flying recklessly into uncharted darkness where you can no longer feel your legs let alone your ass, get paranoid your car may fall apart, "Hold me closer, tiny dancer," Sir Elton blares, as you count the headlights on the highway, and then finally Georgia, the devil has arrived, find yourself a rest stop but mania and anxiety won't let you sleep, only 2 hours away and here comes the sun, stop for gas for the 5th and hopefully final time, you made it to Jacksonville still wearing your winter vest, snow boots, and pajama pants, St. Augustine, Florida greets you, 16 fucking hours after your journey began and you've been awake for 27, but you made it just in time to celebrate Thanksgiving with your child and that makes it all worth it. Now get some damn rest, you crazy fucking animal you.

Kim's Alley Bar

Dear love, I'm trying to reach you with the palms of my heart, where the storms and waves crash when we least suspect it. I'm the boy in the corner with a dunce cap. I get the participation award for messing up. I'm the cornerstone of your madness, the unflinching love your beautiful brown eyes can't keep away from. Yet, here I am, still trying to reach you, somewhere in Florida with punctured lungs, alone, defeated. I must've been in the ring with Ronda Rousey last night, struggling to get through the first round with our relationship still intact. Instead, I'm drunk again, on us. This beer tastes like you, the evil motherfucker. I'll have another sip to keep you in. This cigarette smells like me, making the rounds from bar to bar and waking up at the bottom of the barrel. Maybe this is where our oceans part ways for good, or stay together for another round. I no longer have control of our destiny, nobody was willing to die and make me god with the exception of you. I have no choice now but to kill myself, only so I can wake up and see tomorrow, and roam these sunny streets alone, somewhere in Florida, without you.

Atlantic City Part 2

Hit up the Taj, night out in AC. I'm an observer of moods and faces from the back burner of the casino floor. I see growling pit bosses and disinterested dealers bored out of their skulls. I see European dancers shaking their tits and asses out of sync, delusional muscle-headed security dudes acting like they work for the Secret Service, the old fart bartender asking for his goddamn pen back before I can finish this sentence. And here I am now, at the blackjack table feeling all kinds of blah, dwelling on my problems, drinking a Coors fuckin' Light. Sometimes I like to revel in the corpse of Atlantic City, and piss on it.

New JersEngland

You're seriously doing this aren't you? Ah fuck, here we go. Wake up at 8, head to the CVS, grab condoms, drive to work, get off at 4 to the craziest blizzard Jersey has ever seen, take a blowtorch to thaw out your car, stop by the liquor store, grab a bottle of Fireball and water, get on the parkway, head north 20 miles an hour, Mario Kart ice level type of shit, it's dark as fuck now, bumper to bumper, 5 fucking hours to get to New York, go through Connecticut, stop at Mickey D's for a gallon of coffee, take a 10-minute piss, start drinking the Fireball and drive like a bat out of hell into the New England night, get pulled over on the Massachusetts turnpike, hide the Fireball under the seat, chug 5 bottles of water under a minute while the copper comes over, tell him you're on your way to see Grandma, pull the sympathy card and badge over his head, you're stupid drunk but he lets you go anyway, it's 12AM now and sleep's knocking, you're 2 hours away, you get to El Rancho Motel and proceed to maul her to shreds, own her full lips open and ready for business, 10 fucking hours after your journey began because men in love do absolutely crazy stupid shit for pussy, even in the middle of winter.

There's a Creeper in Your Inbox

She was my type, the prototype, and still is as I type these words as her luminous eyes glare back as I scroll down, zoom in, and stay put. She likes everything I write, adores the rare selfie that I post and retaliates with one of her own, daring me to absorb her, all with a double-tap, cross my heart, burn my soul down to the heathen ground, and exhume evil spirits of past loves. But how do I get in? Her inbox must be stuffed with cretins thinking they can get a piece, but I don't wanna seem like an over-eager creeper trying to get his cyber dick wet. So, I sit back instead, and wait until she reaches out and lures my impatient shark nose with cartilages of her pout.

Going Through Things

I'm not doing good, I'm going through things, but you won't hear it from me, no, I'll keep it quiet, I'll be a tomb and bury myself along with my sorrows, like an ostrich hiding its mug from the world, because I'm above sympathy and beyond reproach, because I'm not doing good, my face will tell you otherwise, my heart will know the truth, my liver will pretend it doesn't know what the fuck is going on and it'll keep drinking nonchalantly, because I have pain that no medicine can subside, like the coldest winter chill, heaven beside me, hell within, because feeling like shit has become an everyday thing and gloom and doom has taken over my lexicon, the pattern of speech aiming to scream for the whole world to listen and know that *I am not doing good.* You can see it in my writing if you've been reading long enough. I paint pictures so vividly the colorblind can decipher the hues in my blues, the charcoal of my lungs. So please, I implore you to pay attention and know, that if you no longer see me around it's because I'm going through things, and you won't hear it from me, fuck no, you'll know it once I'm gone.

Slow Down, Take it Easy

I need to slow down or Imma die as fast as I'm living. My restless bones ache for marathon sex, deep thrust adventures, inventive fuckery and no-holds barred shenanigans to keep 'em breathing. My tired eyes yearn for sunshine to keep 'em awake, in the form of beautiful babes killing me with a smile, calcium in the way of cold draft brews foaming at the mouth. I'm no longer drinking and driving as an extreme sport, I'd much rather grab a roll of Scott tissue paper and shit on myself, 'cause no one's as good at administering a beat down on my ass as I am, a shell of my former self, I'm half of the half of the man I used to be, I'm ¾ of nothing, I find myself chasing unavailable women, just as I find myself unavailable for the ones available, it's just fucking unavoidable, going on drunk Facebook rants about social issues, taking a piss on popular opinion because I dare to think unpopular thoughts, I need to be less of a dick to chop down my ego a peg or two and learn to love a bit more the things that I can control: my future, my sanity, and who I want to be.

A Sexting Buddy

A sexting buddy, a special kinda escape,
a break in case of, a diversion from the monotony,
a normal unordinary smile, someone who'd kiss
away the bad taste in my mouth, someone I can
brag to my buddies about when we're at the bar
drunk and talking all kinds of shit. I'd like a
remedy, an antidote, a goddamn cure. I'd like
someone who understands that "Netflix and Chill"
to me actually means watching the fucking movie.
Somewhat kinda violent like Django and
Broomhilda. I'd love something sideways nutty
like Morrison and Courson. Somewhat something
kinda different from what society perceives as
normal. I'd like someone who is art personified,
cooking pancakes for dinner butt-naked, wearing
nothing but a Smokey the Bear apron as the fire
detectors cheer her on. I'd like a cautionary tale.
I'd love someone who would David Carradine the
fuck outta my existence and take golden showers
on reality shows. I'd really like that. Kinda.

Atlantic City Part 3

Before Atlantic City perished beneath the sands of the Jersey Shore, I was kind of a big shot. The DJs would announce "Ottis Blades in da house!" and I'd get up and wave, complimentary hookah sent my way. I'd start up tabs for somebody else to pay, free drinks all around, pretty girls joined the party and chilled. I was the Dominican Henry Hill in that Copacabana scene, charming fella albeit shitty individual. Nowadays I hear crickets chirp when I sit at the bar, I see tumbleweed fly by greeting my feet, pussy no longer swings by my table and I can finally sit down to write, in peace.

A Couple of Kids Watching Porn

We were a couple of kids trying to figure out the inner workings of our anatomies, my cousin and I, and how the hell women fitted in with such an ordeal. The older kids would fire-up the VCR and lock us out of the room. All we heard was heavy thumping and weird sounds coming out of the females. "One day we'll be old enough to get in there!" we'd proclaim. Needless to say, the intrigue was killing us. We'd stay up past midnight when word got out of the naughty programming on channel 6, but we'd fall asleep on the couch before the show ever came on. It would still be a few more years before I was introduced to the wonderful world of pornography through a scrambled channel, a jail-broken cable box, and the beautiful stylings of the Spice Network, the minute I was glad to find out that the purpose of our hands were not only to eat, but also to jerk off with.

Lonely Guy

I'm a lonely guy, also kinda lovely. I've deprived myself of company because let's be honest, people for the most part suck. They're boring, dramatic, soul-draining, etc. I'm a lonely guy who likes to be alone sometimes except for winter, when equally lonely – and most times horny – women no longer care about my digits, because they know I'll bore them to death with conversation devoid of any celebrity gossip, latest trends, finger-banging escapades, etc. So, I'm a lonely guy, the type of dude who watches strangers' Snapchat stories to sleep. It's like a reality show but with dumber people. But, the truth is, I'm a lonely guy because I don't have you, and my alone doesn't feel as good because you're no longer around to share it with.

Sleepless in A.C

I hate being asleep while I'm awake. I knock out for 6-7 hours at a time with one eye open and not waiting for the sandman, but because peace of mind told me to go fuck myself years ago. I don't really sleep to tell you the truth, I just give my body enough rest to have enough energy to keep drinking, to keep writing, to keep itself moving from one bar to the next, to keep breathing, because I no longer carry dreams since she took them all with her, in a bag tossed over her shoulders like the fucking Grinch with an evil grin walking all over my nightmares and any semblance of sleep I might get at night. Truth is, I sleep better with my kids, and if I happen to be in love with a good woman by my side, other than that it's just lying twisted on a bed that's sick of my shit, and my incessant scrolling before my eyes shut, only to see her, in the fight of my sanity and freedom, solitude and regret, death and rest, the trees are fading, getting the shakes now, last call for drinks, bar's closing down, sun's out, breakfast is ready.

Rejecting Heaven

St. Paul left the keys under the doormat so I could let myself in, and after 5 full minutes of inner debate, that I did. So there I was, heaven almighty! And it was quite the scene! Deceased pedo-popes getting ready to have a pickup basketball game with the KKK! Murderers, rapist, breeders of hate, but they still wouldn't allow in any gays! I also peeped Joseph Stalin having brunch with Genghis Khan, the Führer feverishly thumping through the diary of Anne Frank, Winston Churchill muttering to himself, "What the bollocks did I do wrong?" Harry S. Truman honored for a job well done. Richard Nixon still denying his crooked ways, Charles Manson wearing the bloody glove left behind by OJ. Bill Cosby gleefully serving spiked Jell-O shots while poor Gary Coleman is having all kinds of different strokes. "This is the most boring goddamn place!" I screamed. "This can't be life!" Jesus Christ tried to turn the water into wine but couldn't get permission from his dad! Resigned to my fate I sat on a cloud and looked down upon the earth below, only to see a jubilant George Carlin, in hell, smiling up.

Embracing Hell

I always get myself into these types of things, I thought, as the temperature reached levels no mortal could sustain, but here I was, finally. I must've fallen through a trapdoor somewhere in time, and here they are! The Rat Pack! Undoubtedly the coolest cats in the room, and Marilyn Monroe keeping the ice cubes cold showing off her tush, sharing a couple of drinks with JFK and Joe D. Robin Williams, who got here just before me, went into a routine, livening up the crowd, as the Jimi Hendrix experience prepared to serve up some licks, then I spotted an empty table for two reserved for Fidel Castro and George W. Bush! Right next to Gandhi and Mother Theresa getting it on in the boom boom room. Strangely enough, Jesus Christ was nowhere to be found, and neither was Judas Iscariot. Then I asked for Tupac but Biggie told me the sonofabitch was living in Cuba! Well, ain't that some shit! Still I felt like I belonged, until the devil woke me up and told me that it was time to go. "It's not your hour yet, O, but it will come soon! I have Brittany Murphy in a suite butt-naked just for you! Be patient, breh, and be good!" Ah, fucking hell!

Colored Chalk off the Asphalt

Lift the carpet high and let it fall, a cloud of dust will come up for air, and then we might breathe a little better if the things we hid under there were brought to light. This is for Trayvon Martin, Eric Garner, Sandra Bland, Mike Brown, Freddy Gray, Tamir Rice, dating back to Emmet Till. Black lives swept under, only finding justice in the tune of sociopathic, trigger-happy cops. Dun, dun, dun, another one bites the dust! So, don't get angry when I say that if I was black, I'd shed my skin and camouflage in the safety net of breathing while white. I'd rather disappear until the streets are safe again and we actually follow our nation's forgotten motif that all men are created (un)equal and I'd get to die of old age in the way Dr. King intended, but instead, we have Malcolm X in his grave doing cartwheels.

In a World...

We conquer lands and devour worlds, sleeping in open palms quickly evolving into curled fists, in a world devoid of movie sound bites, black and white films of yore, resilient yet moving at the slow of light years, pentagram-shaped, counting every grain dropped in the soil, grams of flesh, we coil in regret, we're born again sinners many times over, mustached tramps, big and small, mourners of every piece of us dying in a friendly fire, confined to technology, regressing in time back when communication was left to smoke signals and carrier pigeons, now we sit across one another and don't even talk, phone in hand. In a world where war is a necessary evil, we murder our consciences in the name of ancient scriptures and cleanse our guilty hands with the blood of the pure. In a world where famine and hunger are Olympic sports, there are enough plates to go around but never enough food as the rich wipe their hands with the sweat of the poor. In a world plentiful in resources, we're depleted of love, and green's the drug replacing the planet's blue.

And Then We Pray…

Praying – it seems like it's the only thing human beings can agree on. Praying for something magical, perhaps even palpable, praying for something that never comes. Yet, we reserve our prayers for when tragedy occurs, without the faith to back it up, quietly waiting for the next great catastrophe to assault our consciences so we can pray some more. Then grief binds us and we're united for another week until it's no longer a Facebook trend or on your Twitter feed. Then the praying goes silent and the history of violence repeats itself. And so we pray again to deaf ears, pleading with the universe to repair the damage the human race keeps inflicting upon itself, since time immemorial, all the way until that dreary day we'll be knocking on the door of extinction.

Atlantic City, Again.

Driving around the city that left me for dead, hungover, and unemployed amongst thousands of others still struggling to find their footing once again. Atlantic City sees its children fleeting to Vegas, Florida, L.A. and other fruitful cities and states still swimming above sea level and not buried underneath mediocrity and mythology, to save us from desolate boardwalks, cobwebbed casinos, and abandoned beaches, because truth is, we still rob motherfuckers in the inlet and there's not a soul driving down that parkway on the weekends, tolls and cops perform highway robbery as New Jersey paves its roads with the money I'm not making. Welcome one and all to the ghost of Atlantic City, NJ, still haunting the shore, still barely breathing. So please, don't leave us, I implore you to stay, love us, and stick around, come and get bullied in America's favorite playground.

Growing up Without Feet

I'm gonna tell you about a child growing up without feet, a native son of the Caribbean sun. He walks all over the island on scraped hands, the very same ones he sits on hot tin roofs with, waiting for a miracle to fall from above. His legs are grown though, he wears khaki pants and basketball shorts, but he hasn't learned how to walk yet. Still, he lives, he loves, he farts and picks his nose, he watches cartoon blocks in the afternoon, he follows the crowd on feet he does not own, for his mind is not quite there yet, because it belongs to other people who use it for him, people tied and destined to evil deeds. Now, he pays attention in class, falls in love with every girl he meets, sits all the way in the back with the bad kids, and draws comic strips whenever there's a chance he won't get picked on, which is why it was by design when a Pablo Neruda book fell on his lap and he began to read and write, to form his own thoughts, create his own words finally learning how to walk, using his own two feet. That little boy grew up to be me, and then grew short to be you.

       -           For Josh

Women for All Seasons

Women for all seasons, love throughout the winter, sprouting a new taste during the spring, a different essence to gravitate to, resting bitch faces coming and going taking naps upon my lap after running a marathon atop my loving. Women from here to eternity. Women whose lips never break down from overwhelming kisses, nor do they take pauses in-between breaths. Women with a passionate alphabet in their mouths. Women who scream and shout obscenities and dare to flip a frying pan at your head for a good fucking reason. Women who try to settle you down after a long day and give good head for no rhyme or reason, putting the brain to bed – both of them. Women whose fidelity never strays, and you're the one at the end of an expanded tunnel vision with all streets leading to a future you'll work on at any cost. Women who dare to love and learn and fucking listen. Women who know and expect EVERYTHING that you have to give, trusting you deeply, kiss by kiss, inch by inch. She's the kinda woman your sorry ass needs. Everyone else is irrelevant.

A Day Without Poetry

A day without poetry? Imagine that? A day without a circus running through my head, tired balloons and exhausted acts replaying the symphony of my poor man's prose trying to catch a goddamn break. A day devoid of words, 24 hours without touching a pen like an estranged spouse – she has a headache. A day without blank thoughts sliding through my brain, like your average reality whore. A day where I could just sit, stare, pause, and take a goddamn break for once. A well-deserved rest from overthinking and analyzing every minute of my life, narrating every occurrence, every gesture, every voice, and resisting the urge to pen them down like a desperate junkie getting his fix, like the aphrodisiac that'll get me hard throughout the night. And today will be the day that writing will take a backseat, like it or not, in my hands, or so I think, because the second I tried to put my thoughts away this fucking piece came out.

Of Love & Other Dirty Business

Final Round:

The Rest of What's Left

Another First Kiss

A first kiss is the unspoken verbal agreement lustful eyes make before committing to the act. A first kiss is death after life, a point from which we know our way back but choose to ignore it. A first kiss is the uncharted path to paradise leading the way. A first kiss is opening the gates of heaven while holding the keys to hell for another day. A first kiss is to unbutton nirvana's yellowed brick road, rung by rung. A first kiss is a 5-course meal going back for thirds after seconds. A first kiss is the fear of its aftermath. A first kiss is devastation. A first kiss is a muse's coronation and the shelf life of a poet. A first kiss is the most fascinating game of tic-tac-toe ever concocted. A first kiss is an exchange of spirits, gleefully pushing the moon out of orbit. A first kiss is your lips against mine in a battle of wills, going down in defeat, leftovers for breakfast. A first kiss is to disengage war and sign a peace treaty on their lips. A first kiss is getting permission to fly in their airspace and landing wherever you please. A first kiss is turning the theory of relativity on its head. A first kiss is basking in humidity's great miracle. A first kiss is burning flesh. A first kiss is pounding on their breath until their knees have no legs left to stand on. A first kiss is to purge demons off their tongues and laying them to rest in you. A first kiss is to exhale the weight of the world they'll willfully surrender. A first kiss is coming face to face with mortality and understanding that kissing is the greatest ordeal in the known universe, before and after loving you.

Ode to the Girl

Ode to the girl who stole my eyes on a sunny carnival day. She used them to look over my shoulder to make sure everything I wrote was about her. Ode to the girl who has penned over a thousand poems to her name using my hand and undivided adoration. Ode to the girl with the alarming dependency on 5-hour energy drinks, ready to conjure tropical storms in the streets, at the workplace and in the bedroom. Ode to the girl who had me on the treadmill every day while she stuffed her face with sweets and chocolate treats – I haven't seen the inside of a gym before her or ever since! Ode to the girl whose parting words were "You'll die drunk and alone like all your favorite writers!" – actually babe, Neruda died sober next to his loving wife, thank you very much! Ode to the woman who'd sneak up from behind and bite the back of my neck while I did the dishes, took me upstairs, laid me on the bed, made love like a Venus Flytrap devouring its prey, then complained why the fuck the kitchen was dirty the next day. Ode to the girl who tatted her smile on every girl I'd meet, whose mother cursed me out in every language – mostly English, Spanish, and Portuguese. Ode to the girl who netted a Pelé-sized goal inside my heart. Ode to the poetic Trova of Chico Buarque, to the woman of kiss-me lips, Jose Carioca posture, Caipirinha breath, and tangled hair like Amazonian vines. I promise, this shall be the last ode in your honor until the next one, when I hear the solemn breeze sing, O Que Será?

Let's Talk About Sex

Sex is the tool we use in search of a fleeting moment of ecstasy, escaping in an instant, leaving us wishing it'd linger a little bit longer, but it always keeps moving, making plans with other people. Sex is the aftermath of a trashed hotel room, running on fumes after a marathon we walked for miles, leaving us without running shoes, sweating small ponds where fishes inhabit and entire ecosystems come unglued on our fervent lips, pillow talking our way through the motions of an exhausted morning, breakfast in bed, dinner comes early, blood flowing downstream. Sex is the mental state that binds and chains us to other bodies long after they've left, leaving their spirit with us, slipping through our pores when we share beds with the next lover to replace the last. Sex will consume you with voracious intent. Sex dabs in cannibalism and sorcery. Sex is religion in the carnal desire of heathens submitting to its will. Sex is the pinnacle of men, the one addiction only death can help you kick. Sex is synonymous with solitude once it's gone. Sex is what we crave on cold nights when we reach for a soul to keep us warm but there's no one there. And that's when they return, freezing up our bones, clogging up our skin. Sex is us, sex is them, sex is we. And I could go all day coming up with adjectives to make you stay and understand that sex is you, without me.

There's a War Coming

There's a war coming. It might not be today or tomorrow, and probably not the following Monday while we're having coffee, but it's well on its way, we both know it. The truth's out of hiding, the battle lines have been drawn, the collapsing skies have soured and the Earth's core has been shaken at its roots. You caught me in too many lies, those tagged pictures on Facebook know more than I do. I've grown tired of my opinions being discarded and tossed into irrelevancy when all I needed was my lover's ears to listen. Your mouth's loaded with ammo which you intend to shoot and hit with precise aim, every deathly bullet point you'll try to make, going over the things you've readied and prepared to say inside your head, but little do you know that only a handful of those lethal words will see the light of night, 'cause I'll also be ready to stop you in your tracks, 'cause I've also carried resentment and regrets for years, keeping all these emotions bottled up, 'cause I'd rather get drunk, and turn away rather than face your anger and entangle in yet another argument leading nowhere. But now we have another war looming amidst our midst, definitely the definitive one, and no one's getting the upper hand this time, 'cause now we're willing to die and walk away holding on to our pride, with our heads held high as our love bleeds to death in no man's land, waiting in futile agony for a mercy kill.

Ottis's Shitty Valentine

It's just another stupid, mindless day of the year or so I tell myself, where consumerism takes center stage to butt-fuck people, a very special occasion where all of my exes are getting some primo dick and none from me, at least I know they're happy now, at least that's what I like to think, even better if it's me on their minds as they're getting nailed from behind. Yeah I know, I'm horrible. So, I wake up a full half hour before the alarm, the YouTube playlist I left on somehow made its way to Bruno Mars to further kill me. I waddle to the bathroom with my pajamas down to my ankles, avoiding the battlefield of Yuenglings long dropped dead. Come dick to face with the toilet and take my horny Johnson out dressed in morning wood, so I piss all over the seat, the carpet, the sink, until it changes its aim to the bathtub. Yeah, that feels good. Go to the kitchen for some Crunch Berries and I see them all again: the Aussie reaching for her moldy coffee I left up there ever since she left 7 years ago. I see the Mexican watching me cook rice and beans as I make her laugh with my goofy bullshit. I see the Honduran eager to be relieved of stress by being drowned in kisses, fleeting from her husband. I see my Brazilian excited about Taco Tuesday, taking twosies, having sex atop flour tortillas. I see the United Nations sticking its collective tongue out at me. I see myself alone again, and I smile because I've already been to places I never intended to be, and my heart already knows where it's going. Now my penis? That's a whole different matter altogether.

All the Stops Along the Way

I went back and forth on how to write this piece – either a loving poem accentuating all the stops along the way, or a stream of consciousness that'd end long after we did. The one thing I was sure of was beginning where the day started, picking your happy ass up in the U-Haul to thieve you from your parents. They should've seen this coming the very moment they discovered our Six Flags pictures and that their little girl now had an evil "Spanish" boyfriend. Your father died that day even though he was buried many years later. We were all smiles cruising down the freeway to the first apartment for us both, the attic of a townhouse somewhere in Ocean City, NJ where I bumped my head too many times to the tune of your laughs, where we learned to play house and soon after Mom and Dad, where we painfully learned that bills are the root of all evil, and went against the general principle that kids shouldn't be having kids, so we became three, because we could give a fuck less and fucking was all we had to give. You'd cook us your mother's cooking and give us your father's attitude – beef with oyster sauce with a side of what the fuck is wrong with you? We rejoiced in our newfound freedom destroying large buckets of Ben & Jerry's, driving Mario's Kart on lazy Sundays and bumping heads all the way to adulthood, a place with no return trip where I refuse to stay. And so, I'm back in the U-Haul again to pick up memories left down the Jersey shore, to write a few loving lines about us, accentuating all the stops before the end.

I'd Love to See You Again

I'd love to see you again to be honest. It's been 9 long years now and I hold no judgment or resentment over your decision to leave, no grudges or pettiness left over. I'm too old for that shit. I just fucking miss you. I'm not afraid to voice my feelings, you still know me that well. This is why I'm a writer, the same occupation you branded me with back then, and I've yet to make a worthy penny from this futile endeavor. I'd love to see you once and perhaps have those memories of our misadventures come rushing back. Like getting drunk in the casino without paying a cent, winning big on roulette with your lucky number 22, cabbing it delirious around Atlantic City, finding your MySpace page and your song "Keys to the Motel" on a loop, and then later on the ones written about me, the ones I'd listen to just to remember that someone out there possibly might love me still even if she forgot about me. And I could hit you with all the clichés now, then again, there's only so many ways you can write about someone's smile, and possibly talk about how you took my heart and soul down under with you. But that was not the case because they stayed and I used them to fall in love again many years later, looking for a template that could match in passion, color, and width to what we had. I'd just love to see you again, Aussie, instead of imagining you by my window, contemplating on leaving me, handing your keys back over.

I Love How You Selfie

I love how your selfies stand the test of time, sitting perfectly still as your beauty catches up to your pretty, not to mention how your essence distills visage of a timeless aura through camera lenses, tunnel vision of a glowing screen glowing off your glow, which I hold in my hands keeping you trapped between unreadable lines across my palms, where I keep hearting you with a noble heart skipping beats like a pebble through the pond at Central Park, symmetry of the perfect lips, precarious shape of wide-set eyes projecting entire landscapes through their retinas, retaining irises for an instant, staring directly into mine, juncture of a smile birthed at the flash of a click, hidden beneath a face escaping a few precious seconds from duress, stress, and other calamities only she knows, when it hears that sound knowing it's time to reveal itself to the world, announcing its arrival, to look up straight and strike a pose, just as I happen to scroll by and stop for a long pause, double tap one, leaving a trail of heart emojis and a couple of knives to let you know that you slay, and you've made my night for a day, as your perfect selfie steals my sleep and puts me to bed.

Why Are You Forgetting Me?

Why oh why are you forgetting me? Why am I so desperately trying to hold on to the fragile corpse of your memory? Didn't I kiss you enough until you had no lips of your own to speak of? Didn't I give away my love until your bones ached for my thunder? Oh, didn't we withstand countless of monsoons under covers sheltering the many moons we slept under? Residue of tongues tracing skin, lightbulb lights flickering, lovemaking in the making, unafraid hearts mended and fixed, continuously breaking, Marvin, Barry, and Teddy crooning in the night and dying all over again at the thought of no longer putting us to bed before 3AM. So, I'll ask again, babe. Why oh why are you forgetting me? If you're my recurring dream, the one that stops by every bus station hoping to find me draped with yesterday's paper, snoring on a bench, dreaming of us, hoping to find you lying by my side asking if you could have one more kiss to kiss the solitude away, then I'll stretch the back of my hand across the forehead of a fever dream and let you know that it'll be okay, because I'm taking care of you now, while the wind threatens to disrupt my heartbeat while yours threatens to go into business of its own, daring you to forget me after everything I've done, selfishly unloving myself to still be loving you and getting paid with oblivion in return, before and after taxes.

How Much It Takes

If you only knew how much it takes out of me, to verbalize into prose unwanted feelings of love. These fulfilling yet futile rigorous exercises of writing about us. It's a degenerative disease, that regresses my thoughts in time to build something creative that'll take up the inside of a square cut out of a memory. I get a great deal of satisfaction in creating something beautiful celebrating you. Putting together small pieces of our lives to share with the world, knowing damn well I'll be long dead and missing your ass to pieces before and after the last sentence. How fucking cruel. It must be so good to be the muse, that I'm sure of. They don't have a goddamn care to care for. They just sit back and relax, being worshipped and venerated by stupid heathens like us, knowing fully well they still have control over heartstrings they'll never let go of, like an invisible puppeteer only an inspired and broken writer can see, like the 6th sense in reverse. You're clueless as to how much this writing shit takes out of me. Because if you did, you'd be knocking on my door the next time I immortalize you into words you'll never even bother to read, because muses just don't give a shit unless they can love you in return. And that's the way it is.

Her Troops at My Door

And so she came back, knocked on my door and surrendered her troops at my feet. She was exhausted, she wanted a truce, she wanted to wedge a peace flag between our discordance, to calm our flaring nerves and settle the fuck down a bit, and then kiss, and unbuckle, and unhook, and feverishly rise to the occasion for a final last time, where our clothes caught fire upon hitting the floor and we took each other by the tongue, conceding defeat, condensing and melting, evaporating and breathing life into us by fucking, loving, breathing, and sweating ether from our pores, eviscerating the sheets, because a woman who makes love as hard as this is trying to take your virginity even if you've long lost it, and a man who loves a woman in such manner is trying to hold on to her before she's gone, along with the moon befalling on a gloomy sunshine state, and so we fall in love again after 3AM and until the next time we happen to meet.

Something to Write About

In an attempt to start putting down thoughts, I stop and wonder if this piece is worth writing, or if it's just another story for another day, but I go back and forth with it and change my mind only to change it again. So I chew on it a minute, eating the eraser to pieces, letting it marinate and sit still a wee bit longer, then I begin to formulate words, maybe a clever line or two, intentional puns, passages to set my beautiful albeit fucked up prose aflame. Then, I'm all like nah, not tonight, maybe tomorrow when I'm in the mood and thinking more clearly of what I actually wanna say, before deciding if this is a journey worth taking, a piece worth writing, then I go over the repercussions that it might be because the fucking crowd takes everything too literal, then I sit and stare at the paper gifting me the middle finger flipped downwards saying "Fuck me hard, you slut, I'm waiting." And that's when I know I'm ready to write the stuff I keep putting off until tomorrow, today, starting at the very end of this sentence or so I think, we'll see how many people it will piss off and how many will chalk me up as misunderstood.

The College Look

I remember the first time we made love. We stood face to face lying down on the couch. I slid it in, unexpected, welcomed by the short gasp breathed out of your parted mouth, becoming moans after minutes of heavy petting and gentle thrusts back and forth. I had been courting you for months, I fell through those pretty eyes sliced at the corners, cracked open like almonds on the pavement, inviting me to come aboard before drowning. I grabbed the night by holding on to the right half of your bottom lip, the one you've been sucking on since you were a kid and now looks perpetually swollen. It drove me nuts. In addition to your patented "college look" haircut and squared reading glasses, you had so much charm to pick up off the floor and bottle in any way, my girl of pineapple smile and porcupine skin, nothing could touch or hurt you but me back then. We used to bring Saturday nights to its knees away from the crowds, bullwhipping Dad's Ford Taurus around town. You were my girl, the bookworm little Pinay, the nerdiest of the bunch. That's who I still see when I look at our old pictures, even if I can no longer find traces of you when I see you.

Of Bohemian Dress & Bouncy Curls

As the glow of my phone reflects back on my somber mood, dejected and alone, I think back to that distant afternoon to activate the mind and let my writer's block pass through, 'cause reminiscing I've come to realize that everything about you looked so pretty that day, and it wasn't 'cause of the summer light bringing out your facial features in its shine, and it wasn't 'cause of how your flowery curls dropped, bouncing off your shoulders, and it wasn't 'cause of your beautiful flowing bohemian dress and how it made you feel like a hippie from the old country, but everything about you looked so good that day and it wasn't 'cause how you spoke intoned the perfect voice whenever you let one of those radiant smiles breathe, and it wasn't 'cause every picture was picture perfect even if you were next to me, but everything about you looked so damn gorgeous that one day, perhaps it was your aura pouring out of your pores, engulfing my own at every turn, and how your sugarcane lips were enamored with mine, and they wouldn't let them sit still for a second, or maybe it was your beaming eyes x-raying my heart, and how I could trace moonshine and solar flares along with dead and living stars across your skin, sweating out of our clothes, sharing breaths, forging us into one, but everything about you looked so damn near flawless that night, when love made us only to tear us apart limb from limb, only so I could write this nostalgic piece thinking about you many years later.

Not Knowing a Thing About You

Oh, how I wish I could, I wish I could be shot into the stratosphere and disappear into the abyss above, drop off the Earth's mug into Mars' ass, and no longer think about my past or leave a trace of me to find on social media, not a glance of the antisocial propaganda built on hate and greed, deceit and double-standards, of what you do, who you are, and what you should be like, and consume the latest trends by the bucket, inconsequential parades, shallow-minded limbo, Beyoncé wearing Black Panther drab, Miley Cyrus onstage strapped with a dildo and everyone going fucking mad, hop on political bandwagons, get a hairdo like Sideshow Trump, spew evil racist attacks and win all the votes. Oh, unforgettable love, how I wish I could pull a Houdini act and not ever be seen or heard from again just like you have, not a squeak or peek because I can delete all of our pictures with just a click, but only death will take care of the ones condemned to my mind, and maybe then you won't know a goddamn thing about me, just like I never again knew a goddamn thing about you. Oh, how I wish I could.

Another One For Aussie

"When someone asks you what you are or what you do, tell them you're a writer, tell them who you are." And with that she turned me loose, gifting me with the ability to fly along with the confidence I lacked, sitting by my window, dewy-eyed, smoking her cigarettes, shading the neon glow of Atlantic City grey. She smiled and said "I'll never forget this moment, right here with you." We dimmed the lights and made love until the next day, which saw us taking a barrage of selfies before that was even a word. We kissed sorrows at the gates departing lovers have to endure. "I'll be back in a few months, Yogi Mou. Just be patient. I love you." If I had known that'd be the last time I'd see you, I would've taken your lips to a hidden place where forever lasts longer than a week. Now the fleet of time passes by, watching as I get drunk on the beach, paying no mind to the waves of bikini-clad babes crashing the shore, drunk dialing you while walking 20 blocks to hear you say, "Just three more months, I'll be there soon." And that's when "soon" took too long one day, close to midnight, while I was staring at my phone waiting impatiently to answer, your unforgettable voice saying "Happy birthday, my love, forgive me, but I'm not coming back to you." And it wasn't until years later that I understood that you never lied, and the tears I shed on that night were your attempt to find me again, I looked long and mad, unaware that the one place you actually promised to return to was in my writing. And here you are, Aussie, finally home with me.

Are You Okay?

Are you okay? Are you happy with the results your life has flourished? Are you going back into your box and making excuses? Are you fixin' to disappear? Are you going to get drunk tonight? No different from all the other nights before this one? Are you going to scroll your life away? Are you going to throw a fit and deactivate this shit again? Are you gonna try to call for attention like a little bitch? Are you going to oogle at titties on the Internet? Are you fuckin' retarded? Are you gonna be a big boy, tighten up your pants, and confront your imaginary demons? Are you gonna stop thinking about her and the many ways you could've salvaged the relationship? Are you gonna go over and count the many times you fucked up? Because it's always YOU who fucks up? Are you gonna complain about the cold? Do you want your fuckin' blanky? Are you gonna write some more shitty words to make yourself feel better? All "artsy" and stuff? Because it's the only thing you feel marginally good at? Are you gonna make changes and finish THIS damn book? Are you gonna stop chasing people that want nothing to do with you? Are you gonna let your balls drop and get shit done? Are you gonna snap and move out of state again like you did years ago? Are you writing these questions down to put things in perspective? Or are you doing so because you ain't got shit else going? Are you done, Mr. Pussy, feeling bad for yourself? Good! Now you've got serious work to do.

Salads Cracking up

I'm hopelessly in love with you. Yeah, you've caught me. I know that it sounds corny as fuck considering that I've never met you, and yet it doesn't keep me from wondering what it'd be like to be feasting on your lips on breathless sunny afternoons swinging from a hammock somewhere under palm trees, sipping on drinks, laughing up a fresh breeze, looking at our salads bathed in dressing cracking up, and that gorgeous fuck-me lipstick stretched on your smile, showing off your laughter, patiently waiting on a selfie as badly as I am, thinking of what it'd be like to be more than just another follower/friend on Instagram, coming alive in the fleshy gardens of them puckers, kissing dreamy eyes awake, touching your breath as I slide through the gates of heaven and you leave them beauties ajar for just a tad, thinking of what it'd be like to make love to the thought of making love to you, flipping the bird before the sun comes up, watching it take off from our window frame, calling out of work because the morning belongs to us now and we could give a fuck less along with the rest of the day, and I'm madly in love with the idea of us becoming one.

Through the Eyes of a Poet

I'm looking at you through the eyes of a poet, therefore you're fucked. Notice these eyes threatening to fly up and away with your sails, grounded by the talk of your carnivorous lips, stuck on meat-eaters unable to let go of life for a minute, glued to my eager prose like bubblegum blowing powerful bubbles shaping into verses gone pop, gradually going mad like Jesus in the temple – Hold my beer, Judas, I'm going in. And this is where you need to be careful of the things you speak of, because everything you do or say will be used against you in the court of imagination, in the form of poetry, writing, or whatever. I'll write until there's no room left on your skin, I'll decipher scrolls from the Dead Seas off your unreadable irises and tell you how much I want to fuck you in Greek, with a clear mind, a versatile dialect, and a sharp tongue attached to hard nipples like a newborn, breathing in a kiss and scribbling words on forbidden paths, giving headway to the point of no return, luring you into cummin' waves drowning down a one-man army manned by my dick, for I've always been content with a wide smile and a headful of curls, and I've always been a thirsty sonofabitch when it comes to sweet pussy hitting the inbox.

She Loved My Poems but Not Much Else

She loved my poems, but not much else. She loved how I'd paint pictures distilling from her colorful mood swings, throwing frying pans across the room and other things, and not much else. She loved how I'd trace the nuances of everyday drawings from her face for inspiration, talking about the faults she's aware of but couldn't care less about, but not much else. She loved how I loved the look in her morning eyes right before I laid it down, right after she woke up, sending her off to work beaming to start the day, with the car already warmed up and shoveled out of the snow. She loved how my charm wore her panties over its head, and how I'd casually take her smile and tuck it in my front pocket to places where the sun wouldn't follow, long after she'd left me without a candle to hold, but not much else. She loved being my only muse, she hated knowing my whorish heart still kept a well-lit room for someone else. She loved my fingers well beyond writing, how I'd use them in and out of her shaky anatomy, but not much else. She adored the way I'd worship her lips, knowing well that they hid all the roads leading to my condemnation. She loved knowing my addiction began and ended at her pretty feet, at the mercy of a stubborn heart only willing to love the way I loved, instead of me, for just a little bit, and not much else.

A Good Woman

A good woman, a great book to start, seeing us waltz out of a fairy tale to an even better morning, a slice of paradise with extra cheese and other toppings, a nice little home atop a hill somewhere, overlooking shores we've yet to conquer, oceans carrying winds drying our damp threads along with our eyes, shipwrecked by heartache for the last fucking time, a place for my head times two, children running up the stairs, jumping on the bed waking Daddy up, a sunny day without need of sun, watching her dream sunny-side up, genuine and happy smiles cascading down the sunroof illuminating the day, pouring afternoons flooded with laughter, breezy nights punctured by kisses peeling the ozone of its layers, getting our appetite ready for a delicious takeout dinner and Crunch Berries on the rocks for breakfast, unrated home movies still pending, love making love a priority, Hallmark memories framed in time by candid Kodak moments, vintage magical realism of an ageless continent, and to think that it all starts at the top, with an amazing woman and a good life waiting to happen, and that is that.

Love's Evil Magic

I hate how love just drops on your lap, sprinkling its evil magic out of thin air, unannounced and without warning, unaware of the heavy baggage you'd be carrying, having to double and triple bag it so it doesn't break, standing by, seeing you wearing your past like Rebecca Buendía dragging her parents' bones across the courtyard – One Hundred Years of Solitude reference, seriously, really, read that shit – delightfully waiting in the wings to stop you in muddy tracks, in the most inopportune of moments. I despise how love is all like "Whoops! Here the fuck I am!" Smelling all pretty and nice, reciprocated and required, ready to mambo through the night when you don't even feel like dancing. I just absolutely really hate how love grabs ahold of your face, and kisses your hungry lips without a fuck ever given, because it knows that it found something palpable without even looking, sans doubt and uncertainty to put a wrench in its master plans, because it knows that it has arrived, all grandiose in a cloud of smoke directly into the threshold of welcoming arms, and no blade alive could ever cut its strings. I loathe how love always seems to be one step ahead of me, but never when I'm in desperate need of its fine ass to stroll into town and pay me a visit, when the champagne's cold, ready to pop and celebrate its untimely arrival sometime this year or maybe the next, or whenever the fuck it wants.

A Happy Couple

I see them sitting at the bar across from me. I look at them, hoping they don't notice. I ask the bartender for a beer, a pen, and plenty of napkins to scribble on. I see a happy couple sharing laughs, joyfully kissing in-between sips, he's drinking a cold tall one while she enjoys a fruity drink. They are in love far as I can tell, casually distracted from each other's eyes to look at a smartphone's screen, probably updating a Facebook status because that's what couples throttled by love usually do. Maybe something like "Hanging out with bae, he's my world!" followed by a pair of heart-shaped emojis, yellowed faces with bulging eyeballs, signaling that it's in fact real, something I'll never know. He's a good-looking kid for sure, wearing a baseball cap swearing alliance to the Texas Rangers. She's insanely gorgeous, wearing the kinda smile that'd power up a small, impoverished town in Mexico. I see them talking without pause. I look away when I have to, finding myself writing down their faces into prose, because it's what I do. And then, I feel jealousy lurking the very moment I wish that I was in his shoes, after witnessing another kiss, slowly descending into a drunken haze after too many IPAs, realizing there's plenty of room in my heart's landing strip, but not one kamikaze pilot willing to catch a plane and drive it straight to the ground.

Growing up Spanish

Growing up Spanish is rather hard, and I say "Spanish" in the loosest sense even if I've never been to Spain, only so you'd understand who or what I'm talking about. I refuse to use the term "Hispanic" because it was created by the U.S Government in order to classify a whole continent of diverse people and put them in a box. Okay I'm getting all political now – kinda sexy I know – still, forget everything you just read, Latino is a better term to define us anyway. Okay, let's back up a bit, growing up as a LATINO I'm expected to know how to dance salsa, cook some mean rice and beans, dress all rico/suave for the occasion and pack in the bedroom some good fuckin' dick – which I do, wink wink, nudge nudge. I'm expected to fall in line with stereotypes, I'm supposed to be a super macho man, tie my barefooted chick to the kitchen and beat the fuck outta her when she gets out of line, I'm expected to talk fast and act all crazy, speak with a ridiculous over the top accent, I'm expected to know how to fix everything, I'm supposed to be a job-thieving illegal, I'm supposed to be an illiterate drunk, I'm supposed to be what judgmental eyes perceive. So, I implore you to grab your nearest Mexican, get 'em a few Cervezas and get to know us a bit better, before you even DARE cast a vote for Trump.

She's You

She's the sunset crashing down on dawn, she's the mercurial definition of outer space within, she's divine intervention missing all the bullets in my disbelief, she's the heavens in all its majestic glory, she's magnetism pulling beneath my universe's core, swallowing me into the concrete, chewing and spitting up bones and playing guitar with my hapless strings, she's dry mountainous landscapes that blossom, she's snowcaps at night, she's fresh grapefruit from concentrate, not from the carton, she's the one who lands on my heart's Vegas landing strip, she's butterfly lips come alive over crowded sidewalks, she sprouts a pout and spots me a kiss, she's cacti love where a prick easily pricks the finger of a prick by the touch, she's the one who killed the King on the John, she's moon water distilling across the cosmos, she's poetry on a thirsty tongue, she's…you.

MySpace & Yours

And this was it, after months of talking sweet nothings and astronomical phone bills had accumulated to this moment, I was meeting the girl from MySpace for the first time, on my space away from Jersey – New York City. I got off the bus at 42nd and began my search for her in the crowd of the terminal. We had written love letters to each other to trade upon meeting, maybe as disclaimers giving us freedom to walk away if we weren't attracted, because after all, hardly anybody looks like their pictures most of the time, but she did thank god, not as tall as I expected though, but I had already came to adore her wise face and Yahoo serious accent. I made a beeline for her lips the second I saw her, marking it the first time I kissed a woman on first sight, but not the last. We walked aimlessly down the streets of Hell's Kitchen, took pictures with bootlegged cartoon characters roaming Times Square. We made out like teens in what must've been the last phone booth in NYC. I came out of there feeling super to say the least. Then, we hit a Starbucks for whip cream caramel lattes and they fucked up my name on the cup as usual. "Arnold" it read. It didn't matter though; we had found instant love that afternoon. Aussie handed the camera to an employee to take a picture, saying "Do you believe I just met this fucking guy?" She smooched me a kiss at the click of the flash, all smiles, ready to come back home to Jersey with me.

Something to Be Excited About

I'm looking for something to be excited about, a fledging sense of adventure, an unexpected road trip leading nowhere even if we know where we're going, a reason to keep replaying our little adventures inside my head, in places where I can't help you and smiles are aplenty for a couple of lunatics that don't know any better and sights turn genuine and authentic like us, while the cold brews keep flowing and we laugh our lost paths into each other. I don't know crazy love, but I'm looking for something a bit lovely, where every goddamn moon is made of honey and what's mine is yours and what's yours is yours, and we sit at the edge of the world sharing kisses that have yet to come to fruition and the moon threatens to fall and crash at our feet, with no fucking regrets to dwell on, ending dreams made of unicorns and leprechauns, hope and desolation, where your friendship is more than just a mere consolation and the drugs that I need in my life, to learn to love you heavily sedated, yet sober. I need something to be ecstatic about, to see in your eyes everything that I've grown to love in the form of a beautiful/damaged woman that just fucking gets me.

Acknowledgements

Special thanks to Sherlyn Vargas for lending her beautiful for this cover, Gabrielle Ayers for gifting her talent and knocking it out the park, Lucifer's Collection for creating the amazing Bohemian Soul logo, and Christina Hart for editing "the longest fucking poetry collection I've ever edited!" Her words, not mine. Much appreciated my brethren. And least but not last, all the readers around the world. If you picked up a book today you're my kind of people. Seriously, keep that shit up.

Follow Ottis Blades on Instagram and Twitter and whatever other social media outlet happens to be hip at the moment @BohemianBlades

Previous works "Drowning Thoughts 4 The Thirsty Soul" and "Al Filo De Un Verso" are also available on Amazon.

Nobody was seriously hurt during the writing of this book, only my liver.

www.ingramcontent.com/pod-product-compliance
Lightning Source LLC
Chambersburg PA
CBHW031401040426
42444CB00005B/371